A
Rookie
reader

Slower
Than a Slug

Written by Larry Dane Brimner
Illustrated by Deborah Zemke

Children's Press®
A Division of Scholastic Inc.
New York • Toronto • London • Auckland • Sydney
Mexico City • New Delhi • Hong Kong
Danbury, Connecticut

To Carson and Cassidy Brimner.
L. B. D.

For the Grant School authors and illustrators,
from whom I've learned so much.
D. Z.

Reading Consultant

Cecilia Minden-Cupp, PhD
Former Director of the Language and Literacy Program
Harvard Graduate School of Education
Cambridge, Massachusetts

Cover design: The Design Lab
Interior design: Herman Adler

Library of Congress Cataloging-in-Publication Data

Brimner, Larry Dane.
  Slower than a slug / by Larry Dane Brimner; illustrated by Deborah
Zemke.
      p. cm. — (Rookie reader: opposites)
  ISBN-13: 978-0-531-17542-2 (lib. bdg.)   978-0-531-17776-1 (pbk.)
  ISBN-10: 0-531-17542-1 (lib. bdg.)   0-531-17776-9 (pbk.)
  1. English language—Synonyms and antonyms—Juvenile literature.
I. Zemke, Deborah, ill. II. Title. III. Series.
  PE1591.B75 2007
  428.1—dc22   2006024392

CHILDREN'S PRESS, and A ROOKIE READER®, and associated logos
are trademarks and/or registered trademarks of Scholastic Library
Publishing. SCHOLASTIC and associated logos are trademarks and/or
registered trademarks of Scholastic Inc.
1 2 3 4 5 6 7 8 9 10 R 16 15 14 13 12 11 10 09 08 07

"Hey, Little Sister, look at me!"

"I am so fast!
Just watch. You'll see!"

4

5

"I'm quick on my feet.
They're as fast as two wheels."

"I am so speedy my tires make squeals!"

"Swift as a cheetah!"

11

"Snappy as a hare!"

"Run as fast as you can . . ."

"I'll beat you there!"

"Oh, Big Brother,
you have it all wrong!"

"I'm fast, and you're slow. So just move along!"

"Like a bear in winter,
you drag through the snow."

"You simply don't have my get-up-and-go!"

"You are pokey as a sloth!"

"You creep like a slug!"

Word List (74 words)
(Words in **bold** are used as opposites.)

	don't	it	**run**	they're
	drag	just	see	through
_long	**fast**	like	simply	tires
am	feet	**little**	**sister**	tug
and	get	look	sloth	two
are	give	make	**slow**	up
as	go	maybe	slug	watch
at	hare	me	**snappy**	wheels
bear	have	move	snow	will
beat	hey	my	so	winter
big	I	nice	**speedy**	wrong
brother	if	oh	squeals	you
can	I'll	on	**swift**	you'll
cheetah	I'm	**pokey**	the	you're
creep	in	**quick**	there	

About the Author

Larry Dane Brimner writes slower than some authors and faster than others. He has written many books for Children's Press, including *Cats!* and *Here Comes Trouble.*

About the Illustrator

Deborah Zemke has drawn cheetahs, bears, hares, sloths, and all kinds of other critters, but this is the first time she's painted a slug. The illustrator of more than thirty books and the author of five, Deborah lives in Columbia, Missouri, where she races her dog, Abby, every morning.